When ADHD Is A Superpower

Mary Crocker Cook, D.Min., LMFT, LAADC

When ADHD is a Superpower

Published by:

Rp **Robertson Publishing**™
www.RobertsonPublishing.com

Printed in the USA and UK on acid-free paper.

To my fabulous adult ADHD tribe.

Contents:

"Why fit in when you were born to stand out?"
— *Dr. Suess*

Chapter One: Defining Our Terms

There is a wildness, a persistent push to be released from social norms and rules that ADHD people like me are capable of experiencing and work to control.

Mary Crocker Cook

I was prompted to write this book in response to the admiration and genuine joy I feel when I am in the presence of successful people with ADHD. When someone comes in for psychotherapy, and it becomes evident to me fairly quickly that this is the area we may need to explore. I usually know this because I can feel a kindred spirit. It's like recognizing another kid who is playing in the sandbox and I think to myself, "I see you!" The goal of this small text is to better recognize the unique opportunity we have in response to being neurologically atypical, and serve as a resource to share with others in our lives who are impacted by our ADHD abilities.

At some point in nearly every interview conducted for this book, the ADHD adult would say, *"You are asking people who are ADHD to think about their ADHD and I never once thought about it!"* I suppose this was the point for me. I wanted to create a forum to spend a few minutes reflecting on the way we operate, the way we process information, and do this from a curious and sometimes humorous vantage point.

Defining Our Terms

ADHD is a neurodevelopmental disorder characterized by impairing levels of inattention, hyperactivity and impulsivity that tends to begin in childhood and often persists into adulthood. The frontal cortex, the part of the brain responsible for executive functioning, is wired differently in individuals with ADHD. There is under-activity due to decreased blood flow, decreased glucose metabolism (a measure of brain activity), and lower levels of neurotransmitters dopamine and norepinephrine. Medication treats the underlying brain biology by increasing blood flow to the frontal cortex, which is under-active. But treating ADHD is not as simple as taking your pills — especially when pills only normalize your brain temporarily.

The most effective long-term treatment is typically a combination of medication, behavior modifications, therapy, and environmental changes that target performance.

About 60% of children with ADHD in the United States become adults with ADHD; that's about 4% of the adult population, or 8 million adults. This figure is thought to be underreported, though, as up to 85% of children with ADHD are at risk for having the disorder as adults, and only 10.9% of adults with ADHD receive treatment.[1] Most scientists believe adult ADHD remains underdiagnosed because diagnostic criteria for ADHD were developed for children, and because adults with ADHD often have comorbid psychiatric disorders that may mask the symptoms of ADHD.[2]

I want to lead with this fact because the truth is that adults diagnosed with ADHD are fairly rare. This explains why we often feel alone in a room of people and are often incorrectly identified by professionals. In fact, as adults, we are often misdiagnosed as anxious, bi-polar, or with a personality disorder.

There have been many books written on the diagnosis and treatment of adult ADHD, and I have read them all. More importantly, I have lived them all. Here are a few of our challenges:

- Blurting things out
- Clutter leading to mental and emotional overwhelm
- Defensiveness and negative self-talk
- Depression
- Emotional self-flagellation
- Forgetting and losing things
- Getting lost

- Hypersensitivity in relationships
- Impatient, impulsive, distractive
- Losing concentration during conversation
- Messy and disorganized
- Lots of unfinished jobs and tasks
- Often occupied with self or easily distracted, making it difficult to maintain concentration
- One-upmanship
- Organizational problems
- Over talkative
- Procrastination
- Poor time management

If you have wondered if Adult ADHD might fit for you, I would direct you to a hilarious video, The 'Unofficial' ADHD Quiz for Adults, by TotallyADD.com[3]

One of the more obvious of our symptoms is difficulty with our memory, which is often interpreted by people in our lives as a sign we don't care about them. I promise that this is not true. I once heard someone explain our memory this way,

Working memory is like the mind's recorder or sketchpad — it holds all the recent information in your mind driving you to complete certain tasks. It reminds you what you're doing, what your is goal at the time, and which steps you will take to get there.

When working memory is impaired, it's easy to get overwhelmed with thoughts, and for our behavior to get distracted by what's around us. So we might have a lot of trouble remembering what we're doing at any given moment, not what we did, which is why we often go into a room and forget why we went there.

I know this well.

I am the rare female (1%) diagnosed with what was called Minimal Brain Dysfunction in the 1970's, back before the label shifted to the more merciful Attention Deficit Disorder with and without Hyperactivity Disorder. I was not treated with medication and instead received support for my accompanying math dyslexia, called dyscalculia. I was left to manage the accompanying ADHD symptoms through attempts at self-discipline and activities, with varying results. I attributed the social behaviors like blurting, impatience, a verbal learning style, and distraction to character flaws rather than connecting to my wiring. I remember changing schools when our military family would relocate and thinking, *"Maybe this time I will be able to be like other people."* It never worked out that way, leading me to conclude as Albert Einstein said, *"Everyone's a genius, but if you judge a fish by its ability to climb a tree, it will live its whole life believing that it is stupid."*[4]

When I was learning about hyperactivity in graduate school, I was taught that we outgrow it and it is most likely hormonal. It was listed in the DSMIII and DSMIV as a childhood disorder, so I had no idea that "minimal brain dysfunction" was neurological and therefore would continue to impact me into my adulthood.

In my thirties, I had a boyfriend who told me that the relationship would not continue if I didn't "do something" about my emotional lability, irritability, overactive mind... and a psychologist friend referred me to an Adult ADHD specialist. It had never occurred to me that ADHD and Minimal Brain Dysfunction were the same thing, so I was surprised when I received the diagnosis and started taking the medication that changed my life.

I say all of this to acknowledge that I understand at a cellular level the challenges and pain of ADHD. I know what it feels like to feel ashamed of my reactivity, to be unfairly labeled, awkward and socially inept, apologetic, and defensive. However, hyperfocus and sustained energy have also been my friend. As an adult, I have started any number of programs and projects successfully because I find **not** trying far more painful than trying and failing. This is an ADHD hallmark. We are compelled forward... our internal restlessness pushes us toward movement. ***The problem comes when this energy lacks direction, not the energy itself.***

The ADHD population is over-represented in the addiction recovery community, so it is not surprising I am also in long-term recovery. Several studies have shown a strong connection between ADHD, drug abuse, and alcoholism. ADHD is five to ten times more common among adult alcoholics than it is in people without the condition. Among adults being treated for alcohol and substance abuse, clinical peer reviewed studies[5] report the following:

35% of Cocaine Abusers had ADHD
24% of Psychoactive Substance Abusers had ADHD
32% of Cocaine Users and Alcoholics had ADHD
70% of Crystal Meth (Methamphetamine) Inpatients had ADHD

As an addiction treatment specialist, it was inevitable that the presence of ADHD in the treatment population made it a natural home for me, professionally and personally, my entire adult life.

Professionally, ADHD adults are also likely to show up in certain professions like sales, inventors, entrepreneurs, performing artists, graphic designers, EMTs, firefighters, and teachers. Interestingly enough, we are not over-represented in traditional therapist training settings, but I have been able to flourish because I have had the opportunity to teach and train new counselors for thirty years to balance my clinical work. I have had an outlet for self-expression that is necessary for someone like me, but not appropriate in psychotherapy! In addition, the psychology field is multi-dimensional, so there are a variety of ways I can participate and utilize my creativity.

As an adult with ADHD, I am instinctively aware when I am in the presence of another person like me. When I meet one, it feels like breathing because verbal exchanges can be at our natural pace. As a therapist, I feel it before I run through the technical symptom list. It's as though I can "see" them the way I can "see" the substance user and adult child of an alcoholic.

A 2017 Fastbrain posting[6] identified five key strengths of ADHD adults, which I have identified as superpowers:

- Creativity
- Innovation
- Hyperfocus
- High Energy
- Productivity

When ADHD is A Superpower is designed to shift the conversation to our strengths, to ways to view our symptoms to appreciate the way we are neurologically wired rather than self-identify as impaired or "difficult." I have included a list of my favorite ADHD authors in the Index for those who would like to learn more about ADHD symptoms and treatment.

Rather than a list of symptoms to describe us, helpful as they are to diagnosis and treatment, I want to call attention to the reality of being who we are. I am going to do this through interviews with ADHD adults who can share their reality from the inside out. They include an attorney, a financial planner, an MMA fighter, an addiction counselor, a sales manager, a social work administrator, and ADHD friends. The interviews were delightful, as our poor verbal filters can also lead to a refreshing honesty and transparency. In general, we completely believe that we can attribute a substantial amount of personal and professional successes to our ADHD superpowers.

"Most of us have this story of not feeling comfortable because of how you were. Now they call it ADHD. I just knew I bounced all over the place. I'm glad I had ADHD... It's what makes us creative."

Sinbad

Chapter Two: Creativity

"I prefer to distinguish ADD as attention abundance disorder. Everything is just so interesting, remarkably at the same time."

Frank Coppola

Scientific American article[7] provides this definition of creativity: **Creativity is generally the ability to generate something original and unprecedented. The ideas must not only be new and surprising, but also useful and relevant.**

Mental restlessness has been an occasional curse, yet it indicates we are always thinking, seeing patterns, making connections, and thinking outside the box. I am at my happiest in environments where I can be set loose to solve a problem by seeing connections between ideas and situation that others do not see. It means that I sometimes reach conclusions without being able to explain how I "know" something is true. This trait makes me, and other ADHD people, decisive at times; it seems so clear to us! However, because I can't always "show my work," I have had to train myself to explain my thinking in more linear terms to get buy-in from my coworkers, students, or clients.

Our ADHD attorney sees it in her work with conflict resolution:

"I've had clients tell me I am creative and an outside the box thinker in how I solve disputes. I can really hone in on people and read body language cues. I am able to pull information from them about what they really want, about their intent, and then offer a solution that is outside the contract. I make quick judgments based on the way they wince for a moment, or a shift in their body language. I've had people say, "How did you know to ask that question?"

ADHD people may not need more information, and we trust our observations, so having to delay a decision to accommodate other people's need for more data can feel like a waste of time. However, other people need to see our picture in order to buy in, so we need to help them access the information they need to help them see what we see.

I asked our sales manager, *"How do you draw up a sales approach that goes outside the corporate mission and then make it linear to sell it to engineering executives?"*

"I think I do this by asking a lot of questions. You can steer them down the path by asking questions that lead them to believe that they've come into the conclusion on their own. But they aren't really, because you are putting little bread crumbs down the path. So, instead of them taking 27 bread crumbs to come to the idea, you lay 7 crumbs so they come to the idea faster."

Research has found that adults with ADHD had more real-time creative achievements than adults without ADHD[8.] "ADHD doesn't enhance creativity, but people with ADHD tend to be more creative than the average person," Dr. Hallowell tells Bryan Hutchinson for an ADDerworld blog. *"The trick is to turn all those ideas into something useful."*

Our social work administrator observed:

"My creativity doesn't pertain to art as much as being able to take an innovative idea and bring it to fruition and create connections and programs; looking at a need, a challenge, and designing a project to meet that challenge."

I asked her, *"Do you think it's your brain that helps you see those linkages?"*

"I would say one of my superpowers would be seeing shortcuts and ways to build a path forward towards a goal. I don't give up on something, but persevere to see an idea to fruition."

Our ADHD financial planner was able to describe it this way:

"When I am thinking about a certain topic, the creative thought almost seems like it comes very naturally. When I am being put on the spot, and I step into the situation, I look at it, ask a few questions

and then say, "Can we do this?" This actually happened pretty often when I had a software consulting firm. I would sit down with an executive and be talking about what is going on, and suddenly it would hit me, "How about this? Or have you thought about that?" These are people who know a lot more about their company than I do – I am a complete outsider – but that kind of ability to see out of the box was very refreshing and one of the primary reasons they would bring me back just for consultation. Then I took advantage of the opportunity to build a company and consulting firm by pointing out, "If you would like to take the idea forward, the people in the company will not always see the idea." So I was hired to come in and help implement the idea.

It can happen on demand and doesn't require a lot of preparation."

When interviewing fellow ADHD people, more than one person described naturally being *curious* as a positive aspect of ADHD. Curiosity refers to inquisitiveness, openness to experience, a desire to learn, and it may also be a mechanism that allows people to pursue their ambitions and discover meaning in life.[9]

One of my ADHD friends noticed about himself,

"I'm so curious about learning. When I get interested in something I want to learn everything about it. I research it heavily."

I was reminded of a period of my life when I was studying as an Interfaith Minister and wanted to read the spiritual text for every religion available in the local library. And I did; I read every single one of them and drew out quotes about the nature of God from each them. To anchor my learning, I then created a 365-day reader about the nature of God from a world religion perspective.

Another peculiar example of creativity is the development of my beaded tapestry art form. I have been asked many times over the years where I learned to create them. The answer is something many people with ADHD can relate to experiencing. I was in the fabric store and saw a very fun looking circus animal fabric panel. I was making art quilts at the time, and had the thought, "*I wonder what that panel would look like beaded?"* So, since I had a bunch of seed beads from making jewelry, I started covering one of the animals in beads, and I was delighted!

So, I just kept going and ultimately finished a beaded tapestry as a present for my godchildren's room!

One of my godsons asked me for a beaded T-Rex, and after I finished this, I just kept going. You can see more of my work at www.recoverykitty.com. I have created many tapestries over the years, which means I get asked "what are you going to do with them?' Often. There has never been an endpoint rather than the joy of making them, which brings to mind this quote,

"ADHD brains do not adapt as easily: they have their own rules of engagement. They are motivated by their search for optimal stimulation rather than by what others label as important."

Fuzzymama in attitudemag.com

Accompanying creativity is often a strong sense of humor and quick wit, a result of seeing connections and reaching conclusions quickly. It's a survival skill that allows us to tolerate our occasional social goofiness and lack of verbal filter. I recently came across this observation in an AHDH chat room online,

"'You're so funny.' The thing is, I don't even try. Maybe it's the way I talk in race car speed, or the way I change conversations in channel-flipping fashion. One minute I'm chatting about work, the next about what I want to eat, and the next about the dream vacation, or the latest, greatest idea since the iPod."

I can relate to this having been told too many times to count that I should consider being a stand-up comedian. While it is true that I find myself absolutely hilarious, I cannot be funny "on command," which validates the previous quote because humor seems to "pop out" in response to the stimulation in front of me and random thinking rather than considered thought.

Our ADHD financial planner observes her creativity this way:

"As a financial planner, you can see that there are essentially the same set of financial vehicles available to everyone. I am able to use my ability to link various factors together to figure out how to apply which set to which situation and in what sequence. Other financial advisors I work with do not see the picture in almost three dimensions. That's where I see my creativity."

Our ADHD MMA fighter made a surprisingly similar observation:

"In the martial arts world there are so many styles, but the discipline is the same. I might have a group with an 18-year-old, a 12-year-old and a 40-year-old. Other martial arts instructors have the same discipline in Kempo Karate, and they are looking for a structured way to

teach. I can adjust my teaching approach to each age and use their learning styles to be effective.

I seem to able to create illustrating props instinctually, which allows the learner to feel part of the project rather than just a spectator. I can make the complex concepts simple to hone in, to match their energy and personality."

Our sales manager is also able to see connections:

"I have to sell the CFO and CEO on doing a deal and their typical exec response is, "We don't do that." So, I need to put together why we SHOULD do that for the customer and how to accommodate the customer, which means I have to think creatively. I have to convince the board that the revenue gained would be worth shifting the way we operate."

Our goofy ability to be entertained by our own thoughts also can lead us to be non-judgmental and quick to forgive, having been on the receiving end of a variety of judgements others have made about us in response to our different ways of thinking and sometimes poorly considered humor. This same trait can leave us open to unconventional relationships and conversations with people simply because they are interesting, or we find them stimulating. Our parties can include an interesting mix of people!

I came across this funny quote on a T-shirt,

"I don't lack the ability to focus. I have the super mind powers to focus on tons of things at the same time. So take that, boring normal brain people."

I want to acknowledge that creativity needs limits and structure to avoid the tendency toward the "fast start up and petering out" pattern that creates the abandoned fitness, hobby tools, and half-finished projects that litter our homes. In fact, across all interviews, each adult reported that they require deadlines and schedules to complete tasks because being easily being distracted can lead to procrastination. As *Dr. Ned Hallowell*, author of *Driven to Distraction at Work* explains,

"Make friends with structure, make friends with organization. We tend to see them as the enemy because we think that is going to inhibit our creativity. And so we resist structure. Oh no, that's for boring people that have attention surplus disorder. I'm free; I have ADD. Big mistake. Structure, in fact, potentiates creativity. Structure sets you free. My favourite examples are Shakespeare and Mozart — two of the most creative geniuses who ever lived. Shakespeare wrote within incredibly tight forms, blank verse, iambic pentameter, de da, de da, de da, de da. Within that structure he created infinite variety; he created extraordinary variety, but he needed that structure."[10]

While I know from experience that Dr. Hallowell is right, I can also relate to a quote I saw on Pinterest,

"My heart swings back and forth between the need for routine and the urge to run."

Let's explore your creativity with an online quiz, How Creative Are You? [11]

This free Mindtools creativity test helps you think about how creative you are right now. Take it, and then use the tools and discussions that follow to bring intense creativity to your everyday work.

Chapter Three: Innovation

Where does innovation, invention, or creativity come from? Scott Barry Kaufman, a cognitive psychologist and scientific director at the Imagination Institute in the Positive Psychology Center at the University of Pennsylvania, describes it this way[12]:

The brain's default mode network, which controls cognitive processes like perspective taking, daydreaming, and mind wandering, is most active when our mind is resting. And when examining FMRI studies, Kaufman says that this part of the brain is more active in people diagnosed with ADHD.

"I refer to it as the imagination brain network because I think that's what it really is," he says. "The latest research shows that the imagination brain network is highly conducive to creativity and creative thought. And those who are diagnosed with ADHD seem to have greater difficulty than those who are not diagnosed with ADHD in suppressing activity in this imagination brain network. In a way, you can actually conceptualize that people with ADHD have an overactive imagination as opposed to a learning disability."

Many ADHD people like myself have difficulty with boundaries unless they "make sense" to us. Doing things because they have always been done this way is an energy killer for us, and the best use of an ADHD adult is to let us ask "Why not?" and find breakthroughs and work-arounds. This is the trait that leads us to be open to constant learning, preferably self-taught to match our learning pace.

As our sales manage describes:

"We craft deals all day long, and I can see exactly what the customer wants, and I have to sell everyone on my side how to give the customer what they want. I push people's boundaries, 'Why can't we do that?'"

Three aspects of creative cognition are divergent thinking, conceptual expansion and overcoming knowledge constraints. Divergent thinking, or the ability to think of many ideas from a single starting point, is a critical part of creative thinking. Previous research has established that individuals with ADHD are exceptionally good at divergent thinking tasks, such as inventing creative new uses for everyday objects, and brainstorming new features for an innovative cell phone device.[13]

"Individuals with ADHD may be less prone to design fixation, which is the tendency to get stuck in a rut or stick closely to what already exists when creating a new product," H.A.White said.

"This has implications for creative design and problem solving in the real world, when the goal is to create or invent something new without being overly constrained by old models or ways of doing things."[14]

Our ADHD attorney gives a very practical illustration of this trait:

"Billing. In law firms, you have to capture your time in ways to account for it. I ended up being the go-to billing mentor even though it was something I hated. Somehow, I was able to construct a code based on patterns I was seeing over the volume of work. To me, it's not innovative because it seems natural to me to create a system based on patterns."

For other people, it does not seem obvious, but we undervalue what we do because it comes so naturally to us.

"I think seeing patterns is why I am able to handle high volumes of work," our attorney continues.

Our ADHD MMA fighter describes our innovation skills beautifully:

"I am able to create video products by seeing the holes in what is currently being offered. For example, we were doing a martial arts and video with a limited budget, and everyone else had done videos from the left and right side. I wanted to do videos from under and over, so I designed a Plexiglas floor to shoot from underneath. I made the floor and created a spinner so I could turn the platform with my hand while the video stayed stationary; so, the video became 360 degree."

I asked him, "How did you know how to design it?"

"I just visualized it and knew it would work. I could see the whole project. It was hard to explain to people, who told me it would crack, etc. But when talking to the people at TAP plastic, I was able to figure out the exact width I needed to hold 200 pounds while the platform remained clear enough to film through."

Our social work administrator creates stories with data:

"I manually bring the data from different sources to tell a story with data because the system is not designed for the different parts to speak to each other. I take the data and turn it into a narrative for funding and executive management."

A willingness to be brave or to take risks and be responsible for one's actions as we are proposing new innovations relates to *integrity*. Being open about having ADHD makes us feel authentic and honest, which are attributes that characterize integrity.[15] A hallmark of authentic behavior and autonomy is intrinsic motivation. Ryan and Deci said "when intrinsically motivated, a person is moved to act for the fun or challenge entailed rather than because of external products, pressures or reward."[16]

So, it can be a challenge to monetize our work and fully describe what we offer. On the one hand, we can do tasks faster, which may mean an hourly job is not in our best interest. In other cases, we will spend more time than others will because we get driven by our own internal standards or picture of the outcome we are seeking.

Our social work administrator added:

"When we started working remotely, I was furious that I had to keep track of my hours on survey monkey. But as I started to write down what I was actually doing, I was amazed at how productive I really am. Then my manager sent out everyone's hours, and my colleagues noticed that I was working 10 hours or more and hadn't realized it. I am focused on the task, not the time."

Chapter Four: Hyperfocus

"I am ridiculously observant to some things and then completely oblivious to other things."

Kushandwisdom on Twitter

The flip side of a lack of focus is hyperfocus, which is one of our greatest superpowers! Hyperfocus is not, technically, part of the definition of ADHD, but it is widely experienced by those who manage ADHD on a daily basis.

Hyperfocus is the experience of deep and intense concentration in some people with ADHD. ADHD is not necessarily a deficit of attention, but rather a problem with regulating one's attention span to desired tasks. So, while mundane tasks may be difficult to focus on, others may be completely absorbing.

As our ADHD attorney noted,

"I tune everything out and nothing else penetrates my focus. Hours pass, and it really helps me get things done when I am up against a deadline. I have a hard time focusing on administrative things without a deadline, but when I see the deadline looming, I am able to charge though it because I see patterns.

I get a framework, and then I start filling in the sections and work until it gets done."

A Note About Global Thinking

When I designed the program at SJCC, I took a look at the educational content requirements for certification testing. I used them as a framework, and then just built from there. It came easy once I found a framework.

I create material in batches because it easier to manufacture the courses to fill out my framework – and I wonder if it is connected to our ADHD ability to be a ***global thinker***. We see the whole package at once, and then the hyperfocus allows us to stay immersed to create five courses instead of one to address the different sections that seem "obvious" to us.

Our social work administrator made the point this way when I asked her, *"Do you think it is because you are a global thinker that you can hold all the pasts of a clients in mind simultaneously? Some people find this much harder – they can do this track, or this track, but they cannot focus on multiple tracks at the same time."*

"It is hard when you are this kind of thinker, and move to a more global assessment with people who are more linear thinkers. You hit a brick wall, and you have to take down the wall brick by brick. To buy in, they have to see each step.

When you are a global thinker, the individual steps seem less relevant, which is why we might miss a detail. People who start with an outline are more specific, but get stuck when they hit a snag on something specific, and can't see how to move forward. We trust that we will solve it when we get there."

In his book *Thinking Fast and Slow*, Daniel Kahneman makes a distinction between two systems of thinking:[17]

"System 1 operates automatically and quickly, with little or no effort and no sense of voluntary control. System 2 allocates attention to the effortful mental activities that demand it, including complex computations."

Essentially, global learners tend toward System 1 thinking; sequential learners, System 2.

- Sequential learners focus on details and sometimes need time (and support) to see the bigger picture; details inform them about the big ideas; they learn in part-to-whole ways

- Global learners focus on the bigger picture and sometimes need time (and support) to see the details; big ideas inform them about the details; they learn about the parts after seeing the whole.

"People with ADHD often have a special feel for life, a way of seeing right into the heart of matters, while others have to reason their way methodically."
Edward M. Hallowell

As an example, our sales manager noticed:

"I have trouble articulating linear information sometimes, so linear people can't figure out what I want. So, it is easier to do the task myself. An example would be to ask someone to get a piece of paper I need by the microwave, but there are several pieces of paper by the microwave, and the paper I need is actually on the counter by the microwave, so it is faster to get it myself."

It is my observation that, in general, people with ADHD will almost always choose faster over thorough!

Processing time in cognition[18] relates to the ability to process information automatically and therefore speedily, without intentional thinking through. Global thinkers process quickly, and there are pros and cons to this: We may take less time to:

- recognize simple visual patterns and in visual scanning tasks
- take tests that require simple decision-making
- perform basic arithmetic calculations and in manipulating numbers.
- perform reasoning tasks under time pressure
- make decisions that require understanding of the material presented
- read silently for comprehension
- copy words or sentences correctly or to formulate and write passages

However, advanced processing speed may leave us at risk for appearing impulsive and impatient and leave us prone to more simple errors.

Hyperfocus is the ability to zero in intensely on an interesting project or activity for hours at a time. It may be because our brains are less sensitive to a chemical called dopamine, which is linked to reward and attention. The faulty brain circuits can make it easier for us to be distracted and to be hyperfocused. While we struggle to manage maintenance tasks at times, once we have an idea and a plan to go with it, we can be like a puppy with a sock! The intensity of hyperfocus can kick up our dopamine system and we really do process faster. The downside is dropping details at times.

This translates well into completing even tedious tasks like game design, course development, and writing code if it is our passion.

Our sales manager observes it this way:

"The benefit of hyperfocus is that when I am having a conversation with someone who is stuck, I can hyperfocus, drilling down to find the place where they are stuck and then determining what we have to do to solve it. The problem becomes clear and solution is clear, so I then hyperfocus on the solution.

All the junk, or noise, goes away and the problem pops out at me."

Her response prompted me to ask, *"Do you find that the emotional processing slows the processing down?"*

"100%. I am very good in trauma or overly emotional situations, which is great for problem solving."

As I thought about her answer, it struck me that when we hyperfocus on a task or solution we do not always prioritize empathy or compassion. This can create difficulty with family and coworkers who may interpret our task focus for lack of affection or connection.

Some people describe hyperfocus similarly to a state of flow.

Csikszentmihályi and Csikszentmihályi [19] defined flow as a state of intense concentration, energized attention, complete absorption in an activity that "produces intense feelings of enjoyment."

Our ADHD financial planner observed:

"Once I learned about ADHD, I have more control over my hyperfocus so I have less stress. I can use my hyperfocus mode more deliberately and then become extremely productive.

Having the hyperfocus allows me to get into a level of detail and retain that level, which has been very beneficial. I can see things in layers. I can see a process pretty clearly, and I very quickly visualize the entire process. But to explain it others is a different story. It's like when we watch Sci-Fi, they have 3-D projection, and that's how I see a lot of things, but it is hard to explain."

An ADHD friend observes:

"It's like we can see around the corner, and we can predict the future because we can see what might be coming. This can look like we are creating problems or borrowing trouble. In our minds, it is wise to do the extra work up front because we can see the process as a whole."

Our sales manager observed:

"People don't always understand that we need to start working to address the problem NOW because what we do today, and the faster we do it, means the sooner we can reach the longer term effect we are looking for."

Hyperfocus is why we are irritable when our flow is interrupted. It's as though we have sunk into an alternative space and time continuum where we are free from the external constraints that we operate in most of the time. This can happen in our relationships as well, which can make it hard for us to end situations that we need to end. Our normal solution to a problem is to throw energy at it, and our decisive nature can make it hard to admit we were wrong.

Thomas Edison — who probably had ADHD — put all his efforts toward inventing the light bulb, even when it seemed impossible. In the end, it took him more than 3,000 tries before he made a functioning light bulb. But the victory was immeasurably sweet because he had to risk a lot — and fail even more — to make it work.

Here is a lifesaving illustration of this ability from our ADHD addiction counselor:

"Around eight years ago, a friend and I were walking to our cars parked about 10 minutes away. I noticed a person sitting on the curb breathing hard way up ahead of us. At that point, I stopped being able to hear my friend as she was speaking, and she kept poking me, saying, 'Are you listening?' However, I was honed in on him. I took out my phone and dialed 911 without calling. When we got closer, I saw his ears and neck were red. I asked, 'How can I help you?' He couldn't say anything. I said, 'I'm calling 911' and dropped my phone to catch his head as he started to fall back. It wasn't until then that my friend could see the seriousness of the situation. I moved his legs under him and attended to him until the ambulance arrived."

In her blog **Creating Flow with ADHD**[20], Nikki Kinzer rightly points out that while the capacity for Hyperfocus can be seen as a superpower, unharnessed, it can create havoc in our ability to be consistently productive.

Along the way, she addresses four questions you can ask of yourself to determine whether you're likely to find a state of flow in a project. Consider:

- Do you have the tools required to meet the project expectations?

- Do you have the skill required to meet the project expectations?

- Do you have the interest required to meet the project expectations?

- Do you have the time required to meet the project expectations?

Chapter Five: High Energy

"I am not much on down-time. I'm ADHD, and I gotta be moving."
Terry Bradshaw

Our ADHD attorney said it best:

"I just get shit done, high volumes of work. And afterwards, I will look at what I have been produced and think, 'Whoa, I can't believe I did that.' I take bulks of information, synthesize it into categories that make sense to me, and then I'm able to create a new product that did not exist before."

Closely tied to our ability to hyperfocus is the extra energy battery pack that our neurology gives us that can sustain us long into the night. Once we are in our "zone," we lose track of time and even bodily sensation as we are lost in our project. Many ADHD people function on less sleep in general. Our mind is moving so quickly at times that we can trip over our words, have trouble with word-finding if tired, and blurt out our thoughts to not forget them. On the other hand, I do love to move the agenda forward, which is why I am often asked to chair a meeting. I can also teach 16 hours over two days, which is not unusual for people like us!

We take our energy for granted, so keep working like a donkey, not noticing that we are expending a lot of energy. So, it catches us by surprise when five hours have passed and we did not eat or drink, and it hits us that we are tired. I'm always surprised when I am tired. It can take someone outside of me to point out what I have been doing for me to recognize why.

Our ADHD attorney went on to say,

"I could spend hours on a book. I used to get lost in a book and read the entire book in a day. I just blew through them. As I got older, with

*more responsibility, I would feel like I was doing **less** because I didn't have time to lose myself in a book for hours and hours. Now I have to force myself to say, 'Can I do it?' And when the answer is yes, I have to ask myself if it is the **best use** of my time."*

It is possible to have high energy and not have ADHD. The key is people who have attention-deficit hyperactivity disorder (ADHD) are not just very high energy people. They also have severe difficulties focusing their attention and organizing their thoughts. We call what they experience "disrupted executive functioning." Highly energized, active people can usually focus when it is necessary to accomplish a goal.

It is true that there is usually some part of our body moving even into adulthood. For example, I cannot watch television without working on a beaded tapestry or playing spider solitaire. This allows us to complete multiple tasks simultaneously. Athletic ADHD people, in particular, use this superpower to participate in triathlons, competitive weight lifting, dancing, and cycling.

Our ADHD addiction counselor describes it this way:

"High energy is helpful to me when I have to extend myself without notice, and I am able to draw from a well to push myself forward. Whether I need to take on an extra group, or extend my day, I can move forward and not miss a beat. In groups, I think I use my energy to motivate people into motion."

High energy allows us to sustain the energy all the way through.

We measure what we are doing with our energy based on task completion, and other people do task completion based on their energy. The problem is that it catches us off guard every single time we are tired! We are not aware of our physical state.

Our sales manager observes:

"We call it 'deal fatigue' at work. In procurement, the client will blanket you with 100 actions items to go so. Same data on spread sheet 100 different ways. Look, the guy is going to give you 100 things to do and you need to sell to him the way he wants you to sell to him. A lot

of my guys don't have the energy or stamina to get through that, so they get angry, which manifests in how they treat the customer.

I won several deals this way because I just powered through it. And at the end of the day I heard, 'You are the only one who said 'yes' to me and gave me what I wanted; and you didn't bitch about it. It didn't faze you at all.'"

High energy is a symptom that can lead others to issue warnings like, "You are burning the candle at both ends." "You need to slow down and pace yourself," and "I don't see how it is possible for you to do what you are doing."

"Doctors described Jonah as having poor impulse control, which basically meant that Jonah's entire world was a series of decisions that balanced precariously on the razor's edge of clever vs. stupid."

Paolo Bacigalupi, The Doubt Factory

It is true; if we did not have our extra "battery pack", we would not be able devote the energy with the intensity we can offer. I will confess that I have learned over the years to manage this symptom when I am working in a system, like the academic system. The combination of high energy and productivity can cause conflict with co-workers and invite others to want to "partner" with us in order to benefit from our energy and output. It is my experience that partnering doesn't always work well for us if we do not choose carefully as it is our tendency to wind up carrying more of the workload, just because we can. What is joyful is to find a person we CAN work with because combining our superpowers created synergy! I have had that experience as well, and treasure it.

Our sales manager has learned to communicate her reality very strategically:

"I manage 9 guys. For example, we just got a new sales guy, and I needed to show him how to communicate with me. So I said, 'This is how you communicate with me:

- *It's 3 sentences or less, do not send me a page asking me what you want to do*

- *Don't send me a text 100 slides long*

- *Definitely, don't call me, (I don't want to talk to you)*

- *I just want to read it.*

- *Tell me what you want in the first sentence, why you want it and when you want it. If I need more details I will call you.'"*

I asked her, "*How did you start learning to do this?*"

"*I started messaging this when I got into management. I will sometimes joke about it, 'Look, I have ADHD. You have to help me out here and tell me the point.'*

People have to know how to get an A at work, and I need to let them know how to get an A with me."

Our ADHD MMA fighter states it this way:

"*Out of all of the superpowers, I value the extra energy the most. It's like with fighting. You may not be the greatest fighter, but if you can outlast the opponent, you will win. There is no such thing as wearing myself out. My head keeps going and my body follows.*"

Peter Shankman reminds us:

"*Remember that not everyone gets as excited as you do about everything, all the time. Sometimes you'll have to take a deep breath and pause for 10 seconds before you walk into a room so that you don't overwhelm people with your passion, energy, and success. But on the inside, you will know exactly how far ADHD's upsides can take you.*"

Customer Service: New Rules for a Social Media World

Chapter Six: Productivity

"I may look like I'm not doing anything, but I am quite busy problem solving, being creative, or just thinking in my head with 30 tabs open."

Karen M. Zeigler on Twitter

The obvious product of sustained energy and hyperfocus is productivity. Once focused, we can move at a breakneck processing speed, calculating, writing, drawing, problem solving. Our mind is always moving, so the next thought that logically (to us) connects to the next thought will open new pathways. Again, the key is to harness the energy that's the gift of hyperfocus and trust the decisiveness that comes with "knowing" something to be true. Many of us do not have the patience for perfectionism, so once we've completed a project or task, we move forward to the next one rather than picking apart and revising the last one.

Our ADHD attorney noted:

"I can take a massive chunk of information, quickly see patterns, get into a groove, and almost go into machine mode, like spinning a spider web. And it winds up being super productive. All I need is the bone structure of the project, then I can go to town and make it my own."

The ability to distill other people's work and see the overlaps between them, even if they are contributing work from different disciplines is like a Frankenstein -- you pull together disparate pieces of information and it seems to arrange itself in a logical sequence. I used to think of myself as a hack because I could do this, but the outcome of what I was seeing is a unique product."

I didn't realize how unique this is, but it can look slightly magical to people who are more linear and must organize material in a more linear fashion. However, I always need an editor because I sometimes forget to add the connective tissue between ideas. While it makes perfect sense to me that these ideas go together, another reader may not draw the conclusion that seems so obvious to me!

Our ADHD addiction counselor describes it this way:

"I can work through overwhelm and move forward when I have to. I can bust out a tone of charting and then I have a proofreader go through it and manage the detail. While she is doing the proof-reading, I can then produce more completed paperwork! I also use voice texts and emails because I can complete tasks so much more quickly. That means there is occasional autocorrect silliness, but mostly it makes my work flow easier.

Our social work administrator notes:

"Even as a worker among workers, I am still more productive in my 8 hours, not because I am trying extra hard. I just think I produce more because my mind is always working and I manifest. I have to take my inside thoughts and get them out. So, working "normal hours" means normal for who? I could probably do 8 hours of work in 6 due to hyperfocus. Other tasks, I might need more time.

Lunch feels interrupting at noon. I am just getting on a roll, so I forget to eat and take breaks. I focus on getting the task done. I then raise the bar for what I expect of myself."

This made me think of our sales manager:

"I can crank out most things a lot faster than others because I can figure out what is important and what is not.

It can be a problem because I decide as a control thing that I think I can do it faster; I can get the outcome I want. Then I wind up cutting into other people's productivity because I do work for them when I want it done a certain way. It is faster to do it myself than walk someone else through it."

We have a higher tolerance for risk taking because when we fail, we think of another approach or strategy. This reminds me of art projects

I have done where I made a "mistake" and quickly incorporated it into the design rather than start over.

So how do we explain the difference between our inability to attend to some details and our deep concern about others? It is not that we are not detail-oriented – it depends on whether the detail is a reflection of our work or us! For us, it is not about control of other people as much as our need to control ourselves and our work because we are trying to implement the picture we have in our head.

The best use of us is to tell the end the result, and then just turn us loose.

Our financial planner described it this way:

"For example, I took a job with another financial planning company after a certain company did not hire me. In my new position, I reached back out and started talking to the CEO I had interviewed with about market shifts. He started sharing his challenges within his company, and now he is offering to help me in my new position! He had to learn about the way I think, and now he finds it valuable."

Another ADHD friend chimed in,

"However, I get even more productive when I reach out and they are willing to support me specifically in what I need."

It may sound counter-intuitive, but finding a partner is incredibly supportive to our productivity. If it is a good fit, they can fill in the gaps that occur because of our lack of focus on detail or impatience with reviewing completed projects. Because we are less risk-averse, we NEED someone at times to help us see the pitfalls before we step into them. We normally step into them knowing we will find a work around. However, it can save valuable resources to move forward without the potholes and NOT have to expend time and energy in workarounds.

A PRIME ADHD example. I will insert (ADHD) at key places in the story to indicate the superpower involvement.

One of the most productive periods of my life was when I had the opportunity to develop the San Jose City College Alcohol and Drug

Studies Program. I was a licensed therapist and wanted to take classes to get my addiction counselor certification because I was already working in the addiction field. However, the two programs in my area offering the courses were offered through Continuing Ed programs and were $250.00 per unit! This was way out of my price range at the time.

I went to my Dean as a part time psychology instructor and asked him if I could create a certification program that people like me could afford. (ADHD) I did this for two reasons: I wanted to create a stable job opportunity for me, and I really felt outraged that recovering people could not get the education they needed because of money. Community colleges are the absolute best bang for your buck in the world! I had never created an academic program, but thought, "I'll figure it out." (ADHD) He asked me to do a market survey and see if there was a local market.

I did as he asked, met with about 60 people (ADHD), all of whom said, *"Thank God, we absolutely need affordable training."* I reported my findings and he said I could create a course, offer it, and see about the response.

So, I reviewed the educational content requirements of the state certification body and started creating courses using a loose framework of the required content to guarantee their acceptance by students applying for certification. (ADHD) The first class was successful, and he said I could create the other seven classes.

It was at this point I took a risk and said, *"I cannot accomplish this if you make me work with a committee. (ADHD) Our sister college has been writing the first course, as a committee, for three years!"* He decided to set me loose and he remained my main collaborator. I only had to meet with people who were key to the program adoption through faculty senate.

Because I did not have a committee, I was able to complete and launch a completely new certification program in one academic year, which was very unusual. (ADHD) This program just celebrated our thirtieth anniversary! I have created subsequent certifications the same way.

In summary, the only reason I could accomplish this and sustain it is that I had support to do what I felt compelled to do. To this day, I do not know why my Dean took the risk with me, but I will be ever grateful. I suspect it might be because he saw that I would do most of the work. Like most ADHD people, working to the point of over-working is not an impediment when there is a desired goal! It was key that I knew myself well enough to ask for what I wanted and needed, and it was grace that I received it. I ran the program part-time for 25 years and then decided it had grown too large. I then became a full-time Instructor, which, after four years and tenure, enabled me to buy a home. At the end-of-the-day, this is an ADHD story shared by other successful ADHD people I have met along the way.

I ran across a wonderful article by Troy Erstling, *How I Overcame ADHD and became a Productivity Powerhouse*.[21] As a person who has wrestled with harnessing his other ADHD superpowers to become more productive, he offers some hard-won wisdom for being as productive as his energy would allow him to be. Imbedded in each of the sub-headings below are lots of practical and useful strategies that he has found helpful. A must read – and use!

- Minimize input to maximize output — The low information diet
- Busy doesn't mean productive
- Efficient doesn't mean effective

While I am reading this article, I notice that I currently have 10 Word doc windows open and 7 Chrome windows open! This is a common experience for people with ADHD, much like forgetting to close cabinets and drawers once we have found the item we need. This is the same trait that leads us to put items in random areas, resulting in buying items we have already purchased and "lost" three previous times. It is for this reason I have an awesome scissors collection! As I notice all of the open windows, I can't help but smile. Just today, I tried to open my Direct TV on my laptop, and it informed me that I couldn't access it because it was already open in another window! Oops.

Chapter Seven: Optimizing our Superpowers

I have included a variety of wonderful reference books to explore, and as I mentioned in the beginning,

The most effective long-term treatment is typically a combination of medication, behavior modifications, therapy, and environmental changes that target performance.

The key is to find the combination that works for you, and spend the time it takes to design your workflow and lifestyle to best play to your strengths and minimize your limitations. This means paying attention to shifts in your energy through the day which can be a helpful tool to guide you notice what is working for you and not working for you. Because our limbic system, home of the amygdala, is so sensitive we will often feel things before cognitively processing them, so your physical and gut reactions can be a powerful source of information. In fact some people refer to the gut as our second brain because it provides so much neurological feedback. KNOWING without having an immediate corresponding thought is one of our superpowers, so we need to use it for our benefit.

This means that if you abusing substances, or moving too rapidly most of the time, you are not able to hear your internal guidance. Difficulty with impulse control is one of our ADHD challenges, so abusing substances and fatigue will magnify what is already hard for us. It is worth addressing your use of substances and your sleep cycle if you want to fully embrace your superpowers, and I encourage you to give this some serious consideration.

Does this Mean I Need to Take Medication?

There are two major categories for ADHD medications: stimulants (amphetamines) and non-stimulants (methylphenidates). Many adults with ADHD are also placed on depression SSRI's like Cymbalta. The most challenging part of finding the right ADHD medications is deter-mining the right dosage. If the doctor prescribes the right dosage, you will become more focused and less hyperactive. On the other hand, if they prescribe too much of these medications, it can significantly increase side effects without as much benefit. So, if you do go the medication route, prepare to tinker a bit with your doctor until you find the right dosage and schedule for you.

A common fear ADHD people have is that taking medication will damp-en us down, make us lose our edge and flatten our superpowers. In short, we will become "zombies." I can honestly say that I have never seen this effect. In fact, what people say is that they are able to com-plete tasks on the medication before shifting to another task. They are able to manage their irritability when encountering other people who are moving slowly. When medication is working we are more produc-tive and creative and not less so. I know I am able to manage tasks that are incredibly boring, such as data entry for student learning objec-tives (yes, it as awful as it sounds) into the computer system BECAUSE I have the medication support to pull myself forward.

In the end, it is a very personal decision. If you are prescribed stimu-lants, you have an advantage because they leave your system in 24 hours. So you can experiment with them for a week with your doctor and see how they work for you. If they are going to assist you, you will see it pretty quickly. The antidepressant route takes a little longer because it has to build up to therapeutic dosage in your blood stream, but may be the best choice for you if mood swings are a challenge for you.

Final Thoughts

Thank you for spending this time with me. As a person who is often identified as an "energizer bunny," I have found my peace with my ADHD by seeking the gifts found in the diagnosis while controlling the disadvantages it can create.

"... a person becomes a genius to the extent that she stays in alignment with her greatest gifts."

Lara Honos Webb, Ph.D. The Gift of Adult ADD

ADHD is a superpower when we can align our lives and lifestyle as close to our natural thinking process as we can rather than pushing ourselves to adopt the same processes as people we can call "neurotypical," or non-ADHD. Yes, we do like to "see" our possessions, so hooks and clear cabinets might work better for us than drawers. The challenge is to give yourself permission to operate with yourself instead of despite yourself.

Our ADHD financial planner offered this suggestion, which merits more exploration:

"It would be wonderful if there was a way a company could do an assessment and ferret out the ADHD people, who can then be placed in a position where they like the work and their strengths can be utilized and they can do it faster, more creatively, have more interesting ideas... It's like the difference between Steve Jobs and Tim Cook. Tim Cook grew up in an operations, manufacturing background, and is very good at optimizing resources and lowering costs. But you can see their thinking reflected in the products in their company. When Steve Jobs would stand on the stage and present, he could deliver shock and surprise because whoever was working with him was willing to keep the secret.

Some organizations would benefit from restructuring a position to hire for someone who does not have to follow a pre-established process."

Figure out what you are good at and do it a lot! Use the hyperfocus superpower to sustain the flow you feel when you are in sync with who you were designed to be, and then you can laugh when the weirder parts "leak" out.

Another ADHD friend offered this perspective:

"If I had this magic potion that said I would not have ADHD, I would definitely turn it down because I enjoy the perks that come with it. This includes my urge to get up in the morning and get moving. I would never trade it. When I watch people process information who don't have this, they seem so slow. The answer seems obvious to me, but I have to wait for them to get what was obvious!"

Many, many thanks to the fabulous ADHD adults who contributed to this small book written to celebrate us and give us the courage to teach others how best to incorporate our abilities into the work we are called to do. Be encouraged and enjoy exercising your superpowers!

Resources

1. Kessler, R. C., Adler, L., Barkley, R., Biederman, J., Conners, C. K., Demler, O., Zaslavsky, A. M. (2006). The Prevalence and Correlates of Adult ADHD in the United States: Results from the National Comorbidity Survey Replication. American Journal of Psychiatry. 163, 716-723. doi:10.1176/appi.ajp.163.4.716. Retrieved 4/20/20 from:https://ajp.psychiatryonline.org/doi/full/10.1176/ajp.2006.163.4.716?url_ver=Z39.88-2003&rfr_id=ori:rid:crossref.org&rfr_dat=cr_pub%3dpubmed

2. Assessing adults with ADHD and comorbidities. (2009). Primary care companion to the Journal of clinical psychiatry, 11(1), 25. doi:10.4088/pcc.7129bs4c. Retrieved 4/20/20 via: https://www.psychiatrist.com/pcc/article/pages/2009/v11n01/v11n0107.aspx

3. The 'Unofficial' ADHD Quiz for Adults, by TotallyADD.com[1] https://www.youtube.com/watch?v=iozAFIr3BEw&feature=share

4. https://www.additudemag.com/adhd-creativity-brain-health/ Retrieved 6/7/20

5. ADHD Statistics. https://adultaddstrengths.com/2008/10/25/adhd-and-addictions-5-more-clinical-studies/ Retrieved 5/27/20

6. 5 Super Strengths of ADHD Adults You Need to Know (2017). https://fastbraiin.com/5-super-strengths-of-adhd-adults/ Retrieved 4/05/20

7. https://www.scientificamerican.com/article/are-people-with-adhd-more-creative/

8. http://www.adderworld.com/blog1/2012/07/21/exclusive-interview-dr-edward-hallowell-on-adhd-positive-thinking/ 5/02/20

9. Zuss M (2012) The practice of theoretical curiosity. Springer, Brooklyn

10. Hallowell, Ned, M.D. (2014) Driven to Distraction at Work. Harvard Business review Press.

11. How Creative Are You? https://www.mindtools.com/pages/article/creativity-quiz.htm Retrieved 4/05/20

12. We're not doing enough to recognize the creativity in kids diagnosed with ADHD. https://www.pri.org/stories/2014-10-29/were-not-doing-enough-recognize-creativity-kids-diagnosed-adhd   Retrieved 4/05/20

13. https://www.scientificamerican.com/article/the-creativity-of-adhd/#:~:text=Previous%20research%20has%20established%20that,an%20innovative%20cell%20phone%20device. Retrieved 5/12/20

14. White HA, Shah P (2006) Uninhibited imaginations: creativity in adults with attention-deficit/hyperactivity disorder. Pers Individ Differ 40:1121–1131 and White HA, Shah P (2011) Creative style and achievement in adults with attention-deficit/hyperactivity disorder. Pers Individ Differ 50:673–677

15. Carter, Stephen.(1996) Integrity. Harper Perennial; 1st Edition

16. Deci, E. L., & Ryan, R. M. (1985). *Intrinsic motivation and self-determination in human behavior*. New York, NY: Plenum.pg 56.

17. Kahneman, Daniel. (2013) Thinking, Fast and Slow, FSG Adult; 1st edition

18. About ADHD: Thinking Fast and Slow. https://mpmengaged.wordpress.com/2013/04/03/about-adhd-thinking-fast-and-slow/   Retrieved 6/12/20

19. Csikszentmihályi M, Csikszentmihályi IS (1988) Optimal experience: psychological studies of flow in consciousness. Cambridge University Press, Cambridge, pp 5–35

20. Kinzer, Nikki, Creating Flow with ADHD. https://takecontroladhd.com/podcast/373   Retrieved 4/12/20

21. Erstling, Troy. How I Overcame ADHD and became a Productivity Powerhouse, https://medium.com/@troyerstling/how-i-overcame-adhd-and-became-a-productivity-powerhouse-bf-6d4a3dfb51. Retrieved 4/12/20

Reference Book Index

Some of my favorite ADHD authors!

Adult ADHD: How to Succeed as a Hunter in a Farmer's World
by Thom Hartmann

A Radical Guide for Women with ADHD: Embrace Neurodiversity, Live
Boldly, and Break Through Barriers
by Sari Solden , Michelle Frank, et al.

Driven to Distraction (Revised): Recognizing and Coping with
Attention Deficit Disorder
by Edward M. Hallowell and John J. Ratey

The Gift of Adult ADD: How to Transform Your Challenges and Build
on Your Strengths
by Lara Honos-Webb PhD

The Link Between A.D.D and Addiction: Getting the Help You Deserve
by Wendy Richardson

When an Adult You Love Has ADHD: Professional Advice for Parents,
Partners, and Siblings
by Russell A. Barkley

You Mean I'm Not Lazy, Stupid or Crazy?: A Self-help Audio Program
for Adults with Attention Deficit Disorder
by Kate Kelly, Peggy Ramundo, et al.

Contact Information

If you wish to contact me please feel free to call, send an email, or write to:

Mary Crocker Cook
1710 Hamilton Ave. #8
San Jose, CA 95125.

Phone: (408) 448-0333

Email:
marycook@connectionscounselingassociates.com

For more information about my counseling services or presentation topics visit:

www.marycrockercook.com